Why did Jesus have to die?

And other questions about the cross
of Christ and its meaning for us today

Marcus Nodder

Why did Jesus have to die?
And other questions about the cross of Christ and its meaning for us today
Part of the *Questions Christians Ask* series
© Marcus Nodder/The Good Book Company, 2014

Published by
The Good Book Company
Tel (UK): 0333 123 0880;
Tel (North America): (1) 866 244 2165
International: +44 (0) 208 942 0880
Email (UK): info@thegoodbook.co.uk
Email (North America): info@thegoodbook.com

Websites
UK & Europe: www.thegoodbook.co.uk
North America: www.thegoodbook.com
Australia: www.thegoodbook.com.au
New Zealand: www.thegoodbook.co.nz

Unless otherwise indicated, Scripture quotations are from The Holy Bible, New International Version, NIV Copyright © 1973, 1978, 1984, 2011 by Biblica, Inc. Used by permission. All rights reserved worldwide.

ISBN: 9781909919013

Printed in the UK by CPI Group (UK) Ltd, Croydon, CR0 4YY
Design by André Parker

Contents

Introduction

Where can I find more joy? What's the cure for a troubled conscience and feelings of guilt? *How can I get to know God better?* How can I get out of the spiritual rut I'm in? Does God really love me? *How can I grow more spiritually?* Is God really going to accept me when I die? Where can I find the power to change? *How can I become more Christ-like?*

These are just some of the many questions I've wrestled with over the past forty plus years of being a Christian. I'm not the quickest at figuring things out, but what I've begun to realise in recent years is that the answer to all these questions that have troubled me as a follower of Jesus has been right under my nose all along.

What I need is not the latest technique or fad. I need the cross. I need my eyes to be opened more to the wonder of the cross; my heart to be captured more by the beauty of the cross; my life to be shaped more by the power of the cross; my faith to be rooted more in the reality of the cross.

Just a symbol?

If you did a street survey asking people what the cross means to them, unless they've just stepped off a passing spaceship, most would still get the link with Christianity. But beyond that it's anybody's guess. For some, the cross is just the Christian equivalent of the Golden Arches on a McDonald's restaurant—an easily recognisable logo stuck on buildings to tell you where to find a church, if you're that way inclined.

For others, it's a cool design to have tattooed somewhere on your body, alongside a yin-yang or your star sign. Or a lucky charm to hang round your neck, bringing good fortune and warding off any vampires who happen to be in the neighbourhood. Or just a relic of a bygone age, marking the tragic end to the promising career of a great teacher.

If you did the same survey with churchgoers, however, the responses would be equally varied. For some the cross is just an example of self-sacrifice to inspire us to live better lives. For others, it is the place where God deals with what's wrong in the world, but any idea of it involving a sacrifice for sin to save us from the judgment we deserve is dismissed as primitive and immoral.

Or the cross is acknowledged as part of the story, but the real action is seen as being elsewhere—at the incarnation (Jesus being born as a human), or the resurrection, or Pentecost and the outpouring of the Spirit.

Are the answers to those questions of mine really to be found in the cross?

A curious logo

Nowadays, when sports clubs have an animal as part of their logo, they tend to choose ones which are impressive and intimidating to the opposition: bears, bulls, tigers, lions—although in the case of Stockport County, the local soccer club in the town where I grew up, the rampaging lions on the badge haven't helped much (the team languishes in the sixth division).

The same sort of thing was going on back in the first century when Christianity was spreading across the ancient world. Each legion in the Roman army proudly carried the symbol of the eagle. Imagine if instead they'd gone into battle holding aloft a bunny rabbit, or a mouse, or a lamb! And yet for the early Christians a lamb it was.

A lamb isn't remotely impressive. It's weak and vulnerable. And for the Jews, who would celebrate Passover by sacrificing a lamb, it was something you killed. So when those first followers of Jesus found out that he was to be known as "the Lamb of God", questions would have been asked in the marketing department. "Can't we have a lion on the banner instead?"

But a lamb it had to be, because it is the death of Jesus that is central to the Christian message—the gospel. His death *on a cross* no less, with all its associations of criminality, public shame and divine curse.

When John the Baptist saw Jesus coming towards him, he said: "Look, the Lamb of God, who takes away the sin of the world!" (John 1 v 29). And in the last book of the Bible, Revelation, Jesus is referred to once as a lion, but no fewer than 27 times as the Lamb of God. On the throne of the universe, for all eternity, there will be God and the Lamb (Revelation 22 v 1). The angels sing: "Worthy is the Lamb, who was slain" (Revelation 5 v 12). It is as the Lamb of God that Jesus will be known in the new creation, because it is his sacrificial death which is the key to God's eternal purposes.

And that is why the cross is also the key to so many of the issues with which we struggle.

The aim of this short book is that we would understand the cross more deeply, and treasure it more dearly. And that, as a result, we would live increasingly cross-centred and cross-shaped lives, and love and worship more the one who did not spare his own Son but gave him up for us all.

But before we dive into the questions, it is worthwhile reading one of the narratives of what actually happened on that first Good Friday 2,000 years ago...

The crucifixion of Jesus

26 As the soldiers led him away, they seized Simon from Cyrene, who was on his way in from the country, and put the cross on him and made him carry it behind Jesus. 27 A large number of people followed him, including women who mourned and wailed for him. 28 Jesus turned and said to them, 'Daughters of Jerusalem, do not weep for me; weep for yourselves and for your children. 29 For the time will come when you will say, "Blessed are the childless women, the wombs that never bore and the breasts that never nursed!" 30 Then

> ' "they will say to the mountains, 'Fall on us!'
> and to the hills, 'Cover us!' "

31 For if people do these things when the tree is green, what will happen when it is dry?'

32 Two other men, both criminals, were also led out with him to be executed. 33 When they came to the place called the Skull, they crucified him there, along with the criminals – one on his right, the other on his left. 34 Jesus said, 'Father, forgive them, for they do not know what they are doing.' And they divided up his clothes by casting lots.

35 The people stood watching, and the rulers even sneered at him. They said, 'He saved others; let him save himself if he is God's Messiah, the Chosen One.'

36 The soldiers also came up and mocked him. They offered him wine vinegar 37 and said, 'If you are the king of the Jews, save yourself.'

38 There was a written notice above him, which read: THIS IS THE KING OF THE JEWS.

³⁹One of the criminals who hung there hurled insults at him: 'Aren't you the Messiah? Save yourself and us!'

⁴⁰But the other criminal rebuked him. 'Don't you fear God,' he said, 'since you are under the same sentence? ⁴¹We are punished justly, for we are getting what our deeds deserve. But this man has done nothing wrong.'

⁴²Then he said, 'Jesus, remember me when you come into your kingdom.'

⁴³Jesus answered him, 'Truly I tell you, today you will be with me in paradise.'

The death of Jesus

⁴⁴It was now about noon, and darkness came over the whole land until three in the afternoon, ⁴⁵for the sun stopped shining. And the curtain of the temple was torn in two. ⁴⁶Jesus called out with a loud voice, 'Father, into your hands I commit my spirit.' When he had said this, he breathed his last.

⁴⁷The centurion, seeing what had happened, praised God and said, 'Surely this was a righteous man.' ⁴⁸When all the people who had gathered to witness this sight saw what took place, they beat their breasts and went away. ⁴⁹But all those who knew him, including the women who had followed him from Galilee, stood at a distance, watching these things.   *Luke 23 v 26-49*

Chapter 1

Why do we need the cross?

"If there is a God, I reckon he'll be pretty pleased to see me. And as for any stuff I've done wrong, well, God will forgive. That's his job."

An important step in becoming a Christian is recognising how wrong this common attitude is, and how much we do need the cross.

But there's a danger that, as we go on as Christians, we drift away from the cross and operate as if we don't need it anymore. Or at least, not as much as we did at the beginning. If we think of the cross as just a bridge to God, we may feel that now we've walked over to his side we leave it behind. It's done its job. Or we may just feel we're more sorted now and have our act together. Why do we need the cross today as much as we ever did?

The prophet Isaiah was speaking to people who thought they were okay as they were and didn't need God's grace. But then in Isaiah 6 v 1-8 he recounts for their benefit how he came face to face with the reality of what God is like and what we are like. It makes shocking reading:

> In the year that King Uzziah died, I saw the Lord, high and exalted, seated on a throne; and the train of his robe filled the temple. Above him were seraphim, each with six wings: with two wings they covered their faces, with two they covered their feet, and with two they were flying. And they were calling to one another:
>   "Holy, holy, holy is the LORD Almighty;
>   the whole earth is full of his glory."
> At the sound of their voices the doorposts and thresholds shook and the temple was filled with smoke.
>   "Woe to me!" I cried. "I am ruined! For I am a man of unclean lips, and I live among a people of unclean lips, and my eyes have seen the King, the LORD Almighty."
>   Then one of the seraphim flew to me with a live coal in his hand, which he had taken with tongs from the altar. With it he touched my mouth and said, "See, this has touched your lips; your guilt is taken away and your sin atoned for."
>   Then I heard the voice of the Lord saying, "Whom shall I send? And who will go for us?"
>   And I said, "Here am I. Send me!"
>
> *Isaiah 6 v 1-8*

A right view of God and a right view of ourselves are like the two lenses in a pair of glasses. If one or both are missing, things look blurred, and we are in danger of losing our way or falling. But when both lenses are in, our ongoing need for the cross comes into sharp focus.

Calvin begins his *Institutes*, his monumental theology of the Christian faith, with these words:

> *Nearly all the wisdom we possess, that is to say, true and sound wisdom, consists of two parts: the knowledge of God and of ourselves.*

He goes on:

> *Man never achieves a clear knowledge of himself, unless he has first looked upon God's face ... For we always seem to ourselves righteous and up-right and wise and holy—this pride is innate in all of us—unless by clear proofs we stand convinced of our own unrighteousness, foulness, folly, and impurity.*

And that's why we need to start with these two truths. Unless we get these clear, we will never understand why Jesus had to die.

A big vision of God (v 1-4)

Uzziah had been king of Judah for over 50 years and his fame had spread far and wide, but "after Uzziah became powerful, his pride led to his downfall. He was unfaithful to the LORD his God" (2 Chronicles 26 v 16). In judgment, God struck him down with leprosy, and he spent the final years of his life living in isolation. In 740 BC he died, a leper.

> In the year that King Uzziah died, I saw the Lord, high and exalted, seated on a throne. *v 1*

Isaiah was given a vision of the king. The true king. The King of kings. And what he saw shook his world to the foundations.

Majesty

Isaiah must have felt like a tiny ant, gazing up at this throne towering above him, and the Lord God seated on it, high and exalted—in the seat of all authority and power in the universe. Even just the back part of his royal robes filled the temple building. And even the seraphim, the heavenly creatures waiting on God, had to cover their faces from his awesome majesty, like shielding your eyes from the blaze of direct sunlight.

Think of the most important person you've ever met. Perhaps you felt a little intimidated in their presence. But if you'd been with Isaiah, as the door of the temple opened in this vision and you went in, you would have been speechless as you looked up and saw the King on his throne. Breathtaking. Jaw-dropping.

Holiness

> And they were calling to one another: "Holy, holy, holy is the LORD Almighty; the whole earth is full of his glory." *v 3*

That God is holy means he is separate from us and distinct in two ways. First, he is *incomparable*. He alone is the Creator, and everything else is created. As he says in Isaiah 40 v 25: "To whom will you compare me? Or who is my equal?"

And secondly, it means that he is *without sin*—pure, perfect, just, righteous. White-hot purity. In Hebrew one way to express the highest degree of something is by repeating the word. So where our English Bible versions use the term "pure gold" (eg: 2 Kings 25 v 15), the original Hebrew calls it "gold, gold". In Isaiah's vision, the seraphim say that God is "holy, holy, holy". He is the most holy anything can possibly be.

Isaiah was looking at the One whose power is infinite and whose glory fills the earth. So powerful were the booming voices of the seraphim that it seemed as if the building were about to collapse. And smoke, signifying the presence of God, filled the place. Utterly terrifying.

Our ideas of God

People sometimes say: *I like to think of God as…* and they fill in the blank with things like: … *a force like electricity*, or: … *someone who watches over us from a distance*.

This is wishful thinking. It tells you nothing about the God who is actually there, and leaves you with no need of the cross. I personally like to think of my bank account as several millions in credit, but sooner or later fantasy is flattened by the weight of reality.

Here we are confronted by what God is *actually* like— the God who is there. In Psalm 50 v 21 God says: "You thought I was exactly like you". It's a mistake we all tend to make. God is not just a slightly bigger version of us. He is awesome in majesty and holiness, high and exalted, seated on the throne of the universe.

The artist Tracey Emin was commissioned to design a statue for a British city. It was a little bird on top of a four-metre pole. She explained that "most public sculptures are a symbol of power which I find oppressive and dark". She said she wanted something "which would appear and disappear, and not dominate". Is that not exactly what we have done with God? A God of awesome power and majesty and holiness is rather threatening. It's much more manageable to have a tiny God who doesn't dominate. A mini pocket God; a pigmy God; a bird-on-a-pole God that appears when I want him to, and disappears when I choose; a not-so-very-different-from-me God. But the God Isaiah saw is the God who is actually there.

What was it like to meet God face to face?

A deep awareness of sin (v 5)

"Woe to me!" I cried. "I am ruined!"   *v 5*

This wasn't just a "wow", like standing on the edge of the Grand Canyon. It was the "woe" of being terrified. Isaiah knew he wasn't just small in the presence of absolute greatness, but a sinner in the presence of absolute holiness.

In particular, he felt the uncleanness of his lips, and those of his people. Why? Perhaps because on hearing the seraphim calling out he realised he was too sinful to join in. Or perhaps because he knew that what we say reveals what is in our hearts.

It was seeing God in his white-hot purity that made Isaiah aware of how sinful he was. He felt exposed. He was like a bag going through an X-ray machine at the airport; God could see everything in Isaiah's heart. Including all the garbage that Jesus said was in there:

> For it is from within, out of a person's heart, that evil thoughts come—sexual immorality, theft, murder, adultery, greed, malice, deceit, lewdness, envy, slander, arrogance and folly. All these evils come from inside and defile a person.
>
> *Mark 7 v 21-23*

King Uzziah, having been struck down with leprosy, would have had to cry out "Unclean! Unclean!" (Leviticus 13 v 45). Isaiah now realised he was no different—morally. What opened his eyes to that was seeing God as he really is.

In Charles Kingsley's classic book *The Water Babies*, the central character is a boy called Tom, who is a chimney sweep. One day, in a huge mansion, he loses his way crawling inside the maze of flues and chimneys. Instead of coming out down the kitchen chimney, he crawls out onto the hearth of a spotlessly white bedroom, where a lovely little girl lies asleep between immaculately white sheets, a room where not a speck of dirt is to be seen. Tom, the little orphan chimney sweep, gazes around him, enchanted by his first sight of such beauty and cleanness, having never imagined that anything so spotless and lovely could exist.

But then he catches sight of a filthy little creature, sooty black from head to foot, standing on the rosy pink carpet with pools of black perspiration dripping from its body. It is so out of place in such surroundings that he shakes his fist and shouts furiously, "Get out of here at once!" But the dirty figure shakes its fist in return.

And suddenly, for the first time in his life, poor Tom realises that he is looking in a mirror and seeing himself as he really is. It breaks his heart. Uttering a desolate and despairing cry, he rushes out of the house, sobbing as he goes: "I must be clean! I must be clean! Where can I find a stream of water and wash and be clean?"

Seeing God in his holiness is like being dropped into that spotless white room. We suddenly see ourselves as we really are. We look in the mirror and see how out of place we are in the spotless presence of God. We feel ashamed, condemned, afraid. "Woe to me! I am ruined!"

In our worst moments we quite like our sin, but God's holiness means he hates it. It arouses his righteous anger. He *must* judge it. And since we're all sinners, that is a terrifying prospect. The day will come when "people will flee to caves in the rocks and to holes in the ground from the fearful presence of the LORD and the splendour of his majesty, when he rises to shake the earth" (Isaiah 2 v 19). Absolute holiness and absolute power are a terrifying combination.

If we think of ourselves as basically good people, we will never see our need for the cross. But seeing God as he really is exposes what we are really like.

On holiday last summer in Sweden, the sun was up at about 4 a.m. and our bedroom windows faced due east, so we covered the windows with blackout fabric. In the evening the blackout fabric looked perfect, but when a new day dawned there was no hiding the fact that it was full of holes. The sun shone like a searchlight through even the tiniest of them. Similarly, I may think of myself as pretty good, until I hold myself up to the blazing purity of God's holiness. And then suddenly I see how full of holes I am, and I stop comparing myself with others, and say instead: "Woe to me!".

In the chapter before his encounter with God, Isaiah repeatedly says "Woe!" to those who do this, and "Woe!" to those who do that. And no doubt, as God's prophet he was much better than the people he was challenging. But in the presence of God, degrees of sin become irrelevant, and "Woe to them!" becomes "Woe to me". If I compare myself to others, I may think I'm doing pretty well, and I'll be tempted to become proud and judgmental. But once I see God as he is, my self-delusion is blown away, and I know myself to be a sinner. Lost. Ruined. Without hope—apart from the cross.

A transforming experience of grace (v 6-8)

> Then one of the seraphim flew to me with a live coal in his hand, which he had taken with tongs from the altar. With it he touched my mouth and said, "See, this has touched your lips; your guilt is taken away and your sin atoned for."   *v 6*

Cleansed from sin

Under the old covenant, God provided the sacrificial system to make atonement for the sins of the people. But these animal sacrifices were just a picture, foreshadowing the ultimate sacrifice of Christ on the cross.

The coal taken here from the altar symbolised that a sacrifice had been made. Isaiah had confessed he was a man of unclean lips, and now one of the seraphim takes a burning coal from the altar and touches his unclean lips with it. And in that one symbolic act he is cleansed from sin. The seraphim declares: "Your guilt is taken away and your sin atoned for". What wonderful words for Isaiah, or indeed any of us, to hear. "Your guilt is taken away"—your actual guilt before a holy God as well as your feeling of guilt. "And your sin atoned for". Atonement means that the debt of sin is covered, paid in full.

Isaiah didn't say: *Yes I am unclean, but just wait. I'll try harder. I can do better. Give me a chance and I'll clean my act up.* Isaiah is cleansed in an instant—not by his own efforts, but purely by God's grace. And just as he received God's grace through this sacrifice, so as we accept Christ's ultimate sacrifice for us, we hear the same words Isaiah heard—"Your guilt is taken away and your sin atoned for".

This is the only basis on which we can ever stand before God. As Christians we must beware when we start to say to ourselves: *I'm actually doing pretty well now. Been a Christian a few years. Making progress in godliness. Serving in ways I wasn't before. Know quite a bit. And I'm doing more than that person over there.* I need to catch myself, repent of such pride and self-delusion, and see again what God is like and what I am like.

Because even if you're Billy Graham and you've preached to millions, and tens of thousands have been saved through you, without God's grace through the cross, you stand before God today as a lost sinner.

Commissioned for service

By relying on God's grace, then—and only then—we are in a position to be used by God.

> Then I heard the voice of the Lord saying, "Whom shall I send? And who will go for us?" Then I said, "Here am I. Send me!".   *v 8*

Cleansed by God's grace, the prophet offers himself gladly in God's service. And what happened to Isaiah could happen to the rest of the people back then, and to us today. *Woe to me. Save me!* leads to: *Here am I. Send me!* That's the difference grace makes. If I know God's grace to me through the cross, I'll say: *Lord, what can I do for you? How can I serve?* If there's a need in the church, I'll say: *Here am I. Send me!* If there's someone who needs to hear the good news about Jesus, I'll say: *Here am I. Send me!*

But if I haven't experienced God's grace, serving God is pointless and will just make me proud. In the course of a conversation with an older couple who popped by our church, I asked them how long they'd been Christians. And the man said: "Put it this way. I'm a church warden". That's a very common way of thinking—but it doesn't mean anything. I could be doing all sorts of things at church, but never have experienced God's grace for myself. But where God's grace flows in, serving always flows out. And as we serve, we need to keep relying on God's grace and keep close to the cross; otherwise our service will go bad on us. It will become a burden and will feed our pride.

Only if we keep clearly in view what God is like and what we are like will we see our need for the cross. The Puritan John Owen wrote:

> *There are two things that are suited to humble the souls of men, and they are, first, a due consideration of God, and then of themselves—of God, in his greatness, glory, holiness, power, majesty, and authority; of ourselves, in our mean, abject, and sinful condition.*

With those two things in focus, it's clear that the cross of Christ was, is, and always will be, our greatest need.

Is the gospel just another "dying and rising god" myth?

Some claim that the death and resurrection of Jesus is just another version of an ancient myth of a dying and rising god. There is no evidence to support this theory, apart from pointing to supposed parallels with mythical figures like the Egyptian god Osiris or the Greek god Dionysus.

Athens was a very religious city, where people "spent their time doing nothing but talking about and listening to the latest ideas" (Acts 17 v 21). But when Paul came and preached the good news about Jesus and the resurrection there, they didn't respond by saying: *We've heard this one before. It's just another take on the old mythical story!* Instead they called it "new teaching" and said: "You are bringing some strange ideas to our ears, and we want to know what they mean" (Acts 17 v 19-20). If there were parallels in ancient myths, the message about Jesus was sufficiently different that Paul's hearers didn't dismiss it as just another retelling of an old and familiar theme.

Any dying and rising in ancient myths was tied in with the seasons and harvests. The message about Jesus' death and resurrection is unique—that God became man and died for our sins, and was bodily raised to life, never to die again. And it is uniquely rooted in historical, publicly-attested events.

So Paul could say to the Roman governor Festus about the events surrounding Jesus life, death and rising again: "it was not done in a corner" (Acts 26 v 26). The Gospel accounts of Jesus are historically reliable, and testify that he was crucified under Pontius Pilate, and then buried. On the third day he was raised to life, as the empty tomb and resurrection appearances bear witness.

It is not surprising, though, that there have been echoes of this true story since then in various stories, myths and religions. At worst, it shows that the devil is not original, but can only take the truth and distort it. At best, it shows that the gospel addresses needs we all feel. Other stories of sacrifices to appease the anger of the gods point to our common sense of sin and guilt and our longing to be free of them.

Other stories of gods or superheroes rising or returning confirm the universal longing for a saviour and for hope beyond death. And these other stories actually give us another opportunity to tell people the one true story of which they are just a pale reflection.

Chapter 2

What happened on the cross?

What has become known as the "peace symbol" made its first ever appearance on a
London peace march in 1958.

It was designed by British artist Gerald Holtom, who
wrote:

*I was in despair. Deep despair. I drew myself: the
representative of an individual in despair, with
hands palm outstretched outwards and downwards in the manner of Goya's peasant before the
firing squad. I formalised the drawing into a line
and put a circle round it.*

In the famous painting to which he refers, the peasant's
hands are in fact stretched upwards, not downwards,
but anyway, that's what the sign is based on.

For most people, however, that significance is now

lost. Half a century after its creation, this potent ideological symbol has become one of the world's most recognisable designs—and one of the most commercialised. Its creator would surely be turning in his grave if he could see it adorning Tiffany pendants, designer bags, limited-edition VW cars, and Madonna's favourite T-shirts.

Nowadays it's more likely to be seen on the catwalk than on protest marches. And only a dwindling number of people have any idea of its origin in the nuclear-disarmament movement. One creative director commented: "It's become almost akin to a smiley face", which is ironic, given it was designed to express deep despair.

It's not the only symbol to have suffered such a fate. For many, the cross has become just another logo, and they have little idea of its real significance. And even some within the church may feel that perhaps the time has come to get in the marketing experts and come up with something more politically correct than an instrument of torture and execution.

So what actually happened on the cross, and why must we stick with it, not just as the symbol, but as the centre, of our faith?

God gave us the answer 700 years before Jesus was born!

See, my servant will act wisely; he will be raised and lifted up and highly exalted.
Just as there were many who were appalled at him—his appearance was so disfigured beyond that of any human being and his form marred

beyond human likeness—so he will sprinkle many nations, and kings will shut their mouths because of him.

For what they were not told, they will see, and what they have not heard, they will understand.

Who has believed our message and to whom has the arm of the Lᴏʀᴅ been revealed?

He grew up before him like a tender shoot, and like a root out of dry ground. He had no beauty or majesty to attract us to him, nothing in his appearance that we should desire him.

He was despised and rejected by mankind, a man of suffering, and familiar with pain.

Like one from whom people hide their faces he was despised, and we held him in low esteem.

Surely he took up our pain and bore our suffering, yet we considered him punished by God, stricken by him, and afflicted.

But he was pierced for our transgressions, he was crushed for our iniquities; the punishment that brought us peace was on him, and by his wounds we are healed.

We all, like sheep, have gone astray, each of us has turned to our own way; and the Lᴏʀᴅ has laid on him the iniquity of us all.

He was oppressed and afflicted, yet he did not open his mouth; he was led like a lamb to the slaughter, and as a sheep before its shearers is silent, so he did not open his mouth.

By oppression and judgment he was taken away. Yet who of his generation protested? For he was cut off from the land of the living; for the transgression of my people he was punished.

He was assigned a grave with the wicked, and with the rich in his death, though he had done no violence, nor was any deceit in his mouth.

Yet it was the LORD's will to crush him and cause him to suffer, and though the LORD makes his life an offering for sin, he will see his offspring and prolong his days, and the will of the LORD will prosper in his hand.

After he has suffered, he will see the light of life and be satisfied; by his knowledge my righteous servant will justify many, and he will bear their iniquities.

Therefore I will give him a portion among the great, and he will divide the spoils with the strong, because he poured out his life unto death, and was numbered with the transgressors.

For he bore the sin of many, and made intercession for the transgressors.

Isaiah 52 v 13 – 53 v 12

Isaiah chapter 53 is the fourth of five songs in Isaiah about the work of a figure called God's servant. The New Testament reveals that the servant in these prophecies is Jesus. When the apostle Philip came across an Ethiopian reading part of this very passage: "then Philip began with that very passage of Scripture and told him the good news about Jesus" (Acts 8 v 35). And Jesus himself quoted from this passage and said: "This must be fulfilled in me" (Luke 22 v 37).

Of the servant songs, this one is the jewel in the crown. It's very carefully structured, with five sections of three verses each. Sections one and five are about the servant's ultimate victory; two and four are about his suffering; and the middle one—the centre and heart of the passage—is about what happened on the cross. Three themes stand out.

The suffering of the servant

First, the sufferings of Jesus. He's described here as "a man of suffering, and familiar with pain" (53 v 3). He came from unpromising beginnings—"like a root out of dry ground" (v 2). Born in a stable in a poor family, he grew up in a northern backwater in one of the smallest countries in the world.

He was very ordinary in appearance: "He had no beauty or majesty to attract us to him, nothing in his appearance that we should desire him" (v 2). In contrast to the pictures in some children's Bibles, Jesus wasn't the poster boy of his generation. You wouldn't have picked him out in a photo. He didn't have the glamorous good looks of some Hollywood celebrity.

And although at times he did enjoy great popularity, he was widely rejected, even by friends and family. And hated. "He was despised and rejected by mankind ... Like one from whom people hide their faces he was despised, and we held him in low esteem" (v 3). Many hated him so much they wouldn't even look at him.

And this rejection culminated in the appalling physical suffering of his torture and agonising death by crucifixion. "He was oppressed and afflicted" (v 7)—speaks of physical violence. He was so badly beaten that "his appearance was disfigured beyond that of any human being and his form marred beyond human likeness" (52 v 14).

Sometimes you see pictures of someone who has been beaten up by a gang of thugs—their face so swollen and disfigured as to be unrecognisable. So Jesus hardly looked human after they'd finished with him. But the worst suffering of all was something that you cannot see—the spiritual suffering of being forsaken by the Father.

If you want to sell a book on business, the face you want on the front is someone like Richard Branson. Big smile. Flowing golden locks of hair. Gleaming set of teeth. Founder of more than 400 companies. Great success. But if you were going through a hard time, he's probably not the sort of person you'd turn to—unless you were after a handout.

Jesus was not a man of success, but a man of sorrows. And that's important, because suffering is very much part of life in this fallen world. We see it every day in the news, and we experience it in our own lives. How lucky God is, we might think, to live in heaven where all is sweetness and light. What does he know about suffering? **Answer:** *Everything!* The Word who was God became flesh and lived among us. And this God-man,

Jesus, was a man of suffering, familiar with pain. As one old hymn says of Jesus: "Never was grief like thine".

Actors use something called "imaginative empathy". It means that to get into a role they imagine what it felt like to be the person they are depicting. But God doesn't need to imagine suffering as a human being. He lived it. In Jesus he suffered more than we ever will. And that means that when we're finding life hard, we can and should turn to him with confidence. Whatever we're going through—stress, sorrow, physical pain, relationship breakdown, disappointment, loneliness, loss, rejection, betrayal, temptation, fear or bereavement—as we come to God, we know that we will "receive mercy and find grace to help us in our time of need" (Hebrews 4 v 16).

But Jesus' suffering makes him able not just to relate to us, but to rescue us. In some respects the peace symbol and the cross seem remarkably similar. Both represent a man in despair, with his arms stretched out, facing execution. But that is to look just on the surface. God reveals in Isaiah 52 – 53 in what way Jesus' sufferings are unique.

The substitute

> We all, like sheep, have gone astray, each of us
> has turned to our own way; and the LORD has laid
> on him the iniquity of us all. *v 6*

All of us have gone our own way in life, not God's way. Like sheep, we've wandered off from the right path, and that refusal to go God's way has a price tag that has to be paid. In his suffering and death Jesus took on himself our sin and guilt, and took the punishment for it.

Cheryl Anderson was diagnosed with cancer at the age of 32, when she was two months pregnant. With a course of chemotherapy and radiation, she could have survived, but she refused treatment. Her one concern was the unborn child she was carrying. As the cancer spread she was in agony, but refused any drugs which might harm the baby. No painkillers, except paracetamol. She suffered crippling pain, but hoped she would live long enough for her baby to be born safely. Her baby daughter did arrive safe and sound but Cheryl died the same day. It was to save her child that she endured such pain and gave up her life.

Like that selfless, loving mother, it was for our sake that Jesus suffered and died. It was all for us. To give us life. The Bible says: "The wages of sin is death" (Romans 6 v 23). The suffering and death should have been ours. We're the sinners, not Jesus. He was innocent—"he had done no violence, nor was any deceit in his mouth" (Isaiah 53 v 9). Even the robber crucified alongside him recognised that—"this man has done nothing wrong" (Luke 23 v 41). Pilate too recognised that—"I find no basis for a charge against this man" (Luke 23 v 4). Jesus was the only person ever to walk this planet who "did not sin" (Hebrews 4 v 15). With no sin of his own to pay for, in his love he took our sin on himself and paid for them. He substituted himself for us.

Jesus our substitute

The idea of *substitution* is all over Isaiah 52 – 53. "He

took up our pain and bore our suffering" (v 4); "he was pierced for our transgressions; he was crushed for our iniquities; the punishment that brought us peace was upon him, and by his wounds we are healed" (v 5); "the LORD has laid on him the iniquity of us all" (v 6); "for the transgression of my people he was punished" (v 8); "he will bear their iniquities" (v 11); "he bore the sin of many" (v 12). You get the feeling that this is a point God didn't want us to miss!

It's sobering to go back through these verses and change the word "our" for "my". "He was pierced for *my* transgressions, he was crushed for *my* iniquities." My pride, my selfishness, my failure to love God and other people—that's what Jesus was paying for. It's that personal. If I trust in Christ, then I am one of the "many" (v 12) whose sin he was bearing.

But the point is not to make me feel guilty, but rather grateful.

When Taylor Anderson, the child of the mother who died of cancer, grows up, I imagine people will tell her what her mother went through for her, to give her life. And when they do, she will be very moved that her mother loved her so much to do that for her. So we should be amazed along with the apostle Paul that "the Son of God ... loved me and gave himself for me" (Galatians 2 v 20). What's the most anyone has ever done for you? Has anyone else loved you anything close to that?

But the idea of substitution in this passage wasn't a bolt out of a blue sky. The idea of substitution had been at the heart of God's dealings with his people for centuries. At the Passover, God required that a lamb be killed in place of the each firstborn son, so that they could be saved.

Similarly, on the annual Day of Atonement a goat suffered the penalty of the peoples' sin and was sacrificed. And the high priest took another goat, laid his hands on its head, and confessed over it all the sins of the people. And then it describes how "the goat will carry on itself all their sins to a remote place" (Leviticus 16 v 22). So the idea of a substitute was nothing new. The old covenant sacrificial system was based on it. What was new was the sacrifice being a human, not an animal.

In the end it had to be a person. "It is impossible for the blood of bulls and goats to take away sins" (Hebrews 10 v 4). An animal and a person are not equivalent. It had to be like for like. To represent us and take the place of people, the sacrifice had to be a real person.

In the Olympic Games, to represent a country you have to be from that country. And, needless to say, you have to be a person. A cheetah taken from the local zoo would no doubt beat even Usain Bolt in the 100 metres—but would be disqualified for having the wrong DNA. And so, to represent us and suffer in our place, God had to become man. A man of suffering. A real man. "Since the children have flesh and blood, he too shared in their humanity" (Hebrews 2 v 14). Born as a member of the human race. Wearing our colours, and running for our team—Team Human Race. And as a man he suffered the punishment that our sins deserve.

Wicked men did their bit and were accountable for

that, but in the end it was God's doing, and his salvation plan being worked out. Peter says at Pentecost:

> This man was handed over to you by God's deliberate plan and foreknowledge; and you, with the help of wicked men, put him to death by nailing him to the cross. *Acts 2 v 23*

God the Father was directly involved—and this was the worst part of Jesus' sufferings. "The LORD has laid on him the iniquity of us all" (v 6); "it was the LORD's will to crush him and cause him to suffer" (v 10). And as he did so, Father and Son, eternally united in love, were alienated from each other.

Agonising though it was, Jesus, God the Son, was fully on board with the plan. It wasn't a case of "cosmic child abuse", as someone has called it, with God the Father punishing some poor, helpless, reluctant victim. Father and Son were working together. "He was oppressed and afflicted, yet he did not open his mouth; he was led like a lamb to the slaughter, and as a sheep before its shearers is silent, so he did not open his mouth" (v 7). His silence speaks volumes. Jesus, as the good, loving shepherd, was willingly laying down his life for the sheep.

A little girl was playing in the garden and disturbed a bee. The bee chased her, but at that moment her older brother came out of the house and she ran into his arms. The bee didn't give up, and the next moment there was a grunt of pain, and she felt her brother tense up around her. The bee had stung him, and the little girl was safe, because a bee can't sting twice.

On the cross, Jesus took the sting of God's judgment for us. If we run into his arms, we are safe for ever. The wonder of this was not lost on the hymnwriter who wrote:

> *Never was love, dear King,*
> *Never was grief like thine.*
> *This is my Friend, in whose sweet praise*
> *I all my days could gladly spend*

The success of the mission

But suffering and death were not the last word. And if they had been, we would be left wondering whether the substitution had actually worked. Did God accept it?

> Though the LORD makes his life an offering for sin, he will see his offspring and prolong his days, and the will of the LORD will prosper in his hand. After he has suffered, he will see the light of life and be satisfied.   *v 10-11*

After the servant had been killed, how could he then see his offspring and prolong his days and see the light of life? It must have been a real head-scratcher for the first readers of Isaiah, but 700 years later it all became plain. Peter said at Pentecost: "God has raised this Jesus to life, and we are all witnesses of it. Exalted to the right hand of God…" (Acts 2 v 32-33).

That is what we see prophesied here in Isaiah. Jesus was not just raised to life but exalted. That's where the passage begins: "See, my servant will act wisely; he will be raised and lifted up and highly exalted" (52 v 13). These are terms used elsewhere about God himself. He is the "high and exalted One" (57 v 15). What a contrast—the servant goes from despised and rejected to high and exalted. And the risen, exalted Jesus is pictured as a victorious conqueror, returning in triumph from the battle—"he will divide the spoils with the strong" (53 v 12).

When you watch your national team playing on TV—perhaps your football team, or Olympic athletics squad—when they win, you jump up and down screaming: "We've won, we've won!" And yet *you* did nothing. You just sat on the sofa with the TV remote, eating popcorn. But you did win, because your heroes were representing you. When they won, you won; and you share the joy of the victory.

So Jesus is our conquering hero. He won. He defeated sin and death, and he shares the spoils of war with his people. Because of his victory we enjoy peace with God—"the punishment that brought us peace was on him" (v 5); and we are declared in the right with God—"my righteous servant will justify many" (v 11).

Believe it?

They say truth is stranger than fiction, and it is. No wonder chapter 53 begins: "Who has believed our message ... ?" It is astonishing. But everything this passage foretells has now happened in history. The servant of the Lord has come, as foretold. He has suffered and died for sins, as foretold. He has been raised and exalted, as foretold.

A few years after Jesus died and rose again, a man was returning home from Jerusalem, reading this very bit of Isaiah. And he didn't understand it. So God sent Philip, one of the early disciples, to explain to him from this passage the good news about Jesus. And there and then the man put his trust in Jesus and was baptised, on the spot (Acts 8 v 26-38). The message he heard that day is the same one we've heard in this chapter. If it was good enough for that man, why not for you? Or for someone you know? And why not today?

"He bore the sin of many" (v 12). If you are one of the many, through trusting in Jesus, what a staggering privilege. As one song says:

And when I think that God his Son not sparing,
*   sent him to die, I scarce can take it in;*
That on the cross, my burden gladly bearing,
*   he bled and died to take away my sin.*
Then sings my soul, my Saviour God to thee:
*   How great thou art, how great thou art!*

Isn't God unfair to punish Jesus in our place?

It would be unfair of God to punish Jesus, if Jesus were unconnected to God. Then God would be punishing some poor individual who just happened to be in the wrong place at the wrong time. But in the person of his Son, God was taking the punishment on himself. Jesus is fully God—the eternal Word, who was with God and was God (John 1 v 1).

One of the villains of church history is a man called Arius, who was a church leader in Egypt in the fourth century. He taught that Jesus was not God, but just a created being, as Jehovah's Witnesses teach today. One of the heroes of church history is a fourth-century bishop called Athanasius, who made it his life's work to oppose this false teaching, and was exiled for 17 years for his troubles.

He fought so hard for the deity of Christ to be recognised because he saw that our salvation depends on it. If Jesus were not God, then his death could not save us. The biblical truth which Athanasius championed is summed up in the words of the Nicene Creed: "We believe … in one Lord Jesus Christ … true God from true God … of one substance with the Father … For us men and for our salvation he came down from heaven."

But Jesus' sacrifice would also be invalid if he were unconnected to us. If he were just some divine spirit, then he couldn't represent human beings and die for us. But Jesus was fully man as well as fully God. "The Word became flesh and made his dwelling among us" (John 1 v 14).

Chapter 3

Why did Jesus have to suffer?

osts are rising—gas, electricity, food, insurance—and understandably many are worried about how they're going to pay the bills at the end of the month. The cost of living is a big concern, but what about the cost of sinning—the cost of living as we see fit in God's world?

What does it all cost?

Some think there's no cost at all. Live as you want and there'll be nothing to pay—no calling to account. Others think that if there is a price to pay at the end of our lives, it will be negligible. The equivalent of a parking ticket or a slap on the wrist.

In Mark chapter 15 we see the real cost of sinning, in the sufferings of Jesus. The story is told in an almost matter-of-fact way. But it's worth reading again and thinking about the pain and brutality of it all...

Wanting to satisfy the crowd, Pilate released Barabbas to them. He had Jesus flogged, and handed him over to be crucified.

The soldiers led Jesus away into the palace (that is, the Praetorium) and called together the whole company of soldiers. They put a purple robe on him, then twisted together a crown of thorns and set it on him. And they began to call out to him, "Hail, king of the Jews!" Again and again they struck him on the head with a staff and spat on him. Falling on their knees, they paid homage to him. And when they had mocked him, they took off the purple robe and put his own clothes on him. Then they led him out to crucify him.

A certain man from Cyrene, Simon, the father of Alexander and Rufus, was passing by on his way in from the country, and they forced him to carry the cross. They brought Jesus to the place called Golgotha (which means "the place of the skull"). Then they offered him wine mixed with myrrh, but he did not take it. And they crucified him. Dividing up his clothes, they cast lots to see what each would get.

It was nine in the morning when they crucified him. The written notice of the charge against him read: THE KING OF THE JEWS.

They crucified two rebels with him, one on his right and one on his left. Those who passed by hurled insults at him, shaking their heads and saying, "So! You who are going to destroy the temple and build it in three days, come down from the cross and save yourself!" In the same way the chief priests and the teachers of the law mocked him among themselves. "He saved others," they said, "but he can't save himself! Let this Messiah, this king of Israel, come down now from the cross, that we may see and believe." Those crucified with him also heaped insults on him.

At noon, darkness came over the whole land until three in the afternoon. And at three in the afternoon Jesus cried out in a loud voice, *"Eloi, Eloi, lema sabachthani?"* (which means "My God, my God, why have you forsaken me?").

When some of those standing near heard this, they said, "Listen, he's calling Elijah."

Someone ran, filled a sponge with wine vinegar, put it on a staff, and offered it to Jesus to drink. "Now leave him alone. Let's see if Elijah comes to take him down," he said.

With a loud cry, Jesus breathed his last.

The curtain of the temple was torn in two from top to bottom. And when the centurion, who stood there in front of Jesus, saw how he died, he said, "Surely this man was the Son of God!"

Some women were watching from a distance. Among them were Mary Magdalene, Mary the mother of James the younger and of Joseph, and Salome. In Galilee these women had followed him and cared for his needs. Many other women who had come up with him to Jerusalem were also there.   *Mark 15 v 15-41*

In this, the climax of Mark's Gospel, Jesus—the Christ, the Son of God—is paying for sin. Not for his own, because he didn't have any, but for the sin of his people. Jesus said that he came "to give his life as a ransom for many" (Mark 10 v 45). He, the sinless Son of God, was taking on himself the sin of his people and paying for it. So if we want to work out the cost of sinning, we need only look at the sufferings of Jesus.

There's a Christian song that joyfully declares: "The price is paid". Appreciating how high that price really was is the key to so many things in the Christian life. This passage helps us do that.

- For the person who thinks there is no cost to living as they want, this passage raises the question: *Why, if that were the case, would God have allowed his Son to suffer like this?*

- For the person who recognises there is a cost but whose attitude is: "I will pay for my sins myself", this passage is a reality check. *This is what it is like to pay for sin.*

Previously, Jesus had said ominously that he "must suffer many things" (Mark 8 v 31). In this passage we see what he meant.

One experiment I remember from doing chemistry at school was chromatography. Chromatography is a method for separating and analysing complex mixtures. You put some black ink on a filter paper and suspend it in water. As the water is absorbed up the strip, the ink separates into the different bands of colour from which it's made up. When you think about the suffering of Jesus, it similarly separates out into three main bands.

1. The physical suffering of Jesus

First, there was the physical suffering, which began with Jesus being flogged (Mark 10 v 15). This was a horrific Roman punishment in which the victim was beaten by a number of soldiers taking turns until his flesh hung in bleeding shreds. The instrument used was a whip made of leather thongs to which pieces of bone or lead were attached. Often men died from such flogging.

In verses 16-20 Jesus was then subjected to further torture by the soldiers before being led out to be crucified. Normally the victim would carry his own cross-piece (the horizontal beam), but they forced someone else to carry it for Jesus (v 21), presumably because he was already so weakened from the flogging that he was unable to do it himself.

> Then they offered him wine mixed with myrrh,
> but he did not take it.   *v 23*

This was a narcotic drink—an anaesthetic offered to the condemned to make them drowsy. But Jesus refused any painkillers. He chose to endure this physical agony fully conscious.

> And they crucified him.   *v 24*

Crucifixion was one of the cruelest forms of punishment ever conceived. The Jewish historian Josephus described it as "the most wretched of all ways of dying". The English word "excruciating" comes from "crucifixion".

Jesus was stretched out and nailed to the horizontal beam through his wrists. This was then lifted up and fastened to the upright beam. His feet were then nailed in place as well. Death usually came by exhaustion and suffocation.

In his account Mark didn't go into graphic detail about the physical suffering, because he didn't need to. His first readers were familiar with these things. When the film *The Passion of the Christ* came out I went to see it with a friend who is not a believer. He was a pretty tough guy, self-confident, always had something to say. But as we walked out of the cinema he didn't say a word. I finally asked him what he made of it. He simply said: "That was the most powerful film I've ever seen".

For him the cross had been just a piece of jewellery, removed from its context. For the first time he appreciated something of what Jesus suffered physically.

But why in God's salvation plan did Jesus have to suffer so much physically? The answer is that the penalty for sin has a physical dimension. Physical suffering is part of the cost of sinning. And so when Jesus suffered in our place, the price he paid included that. We get a glimpse of this physical cost of sin in our world today. We live in a world in which there is so much physical suffering: violence, abuse, hunger, disease, death. Ultimately, the root cause is sin and God's judgment on it.

But this physical cost of sin will be seen most starkly in the world to come. Jesus warned about a place where "the worms that eat them do not die, and the fire is not quenched." (9 v 48). We could debate how literally we are to take those descriptions, but what is clear from the Bible is that hell is a physical reality. One day, everyone will be physically raised from the dead, either for life with God or for condemnation. Hell is a place of physical suffering.

But wonderfully, because Jesus suffered this as our substitute, we don't have to. Those who trust in Jesus will eventually enjoy life in a perfect world where there'll be no physical suffering anymore—"no more death or mourning or crying or pain" (Revelation 21 v 4)—because that price for sin has been paid in full by Jesus.

2. The social suffering of Jesus

The second dimension of Jesus' suffering was social. This is a scene filled with **shame and humiliation**. Death by crucifixion involved being stripped naked— the soldiers gambled for Jesus' clothing (Mark 15 v 24)—being stretched out and publicly exposed. It was the most shameful and humiliating way to die. And the site of the crucifixion, Golgotha (v 22), was a very public place—a small hill just outside the city walls.

The Roman writer Cicero said that "Even the mere word 'cross' must remain far away, not only from the lips of the citizens of Rome, but also from their thoughts, their eyes, their ears", such was the shame associated with it.

Then there was the **mocking**. Mark 15 v 29-32 describes four groups who ridiculed Jesus as he hung there:

"Those who passed by hurled insults at him" (v 29)—

there were plenty of *passers-by*. "Come down from the cross and save yourself!"

"In the same way the *chief priests and teachers of the law* mocked him among themselves. 'He saved others', they said, 'but he can't save himself!'" Unbelievable cruelty.

"Those crucified with him also heaped insults on him" (v 32). Even the *condemned criminals* raged against him.

And the ruling *Roman authorities* joined in with the mockery. Above his head "the written notice of the charge against him read: THE KING OF THE JEWS" (v 26). It was meant as a cruel joke.

And there was the **isolation**. Almost everyone was against him. He was utterly alone—the object of such venom and hatred.

Why in God's salvation plan did Jesus have to suffer such dishonour and shame and mocking and hatred and isolation? Because that is part of the cost of sin. It was one the "many things" the Son of God had to suffer if he was to pay the price for our sin.

We get a glimpse of this "social cost of sinning" in our world today. One of the consequences of our rejection of God is that our world is filled with so many broken relationships and all the pain and misery that brings. So much hatred and shame and loneliness and social breakdown and abuse.

But this social cost of sin will be seen most starkly in hell. Sometimes people joke that they don't mind going to hell because all their friends will be there and it'll be one long party. But hell is a place of total social breakdown. People will be shamed and humiliated, as

Jesus was. People will be lonely, totally isolated, as Jesus was. There'll be no love or friendship—just hatred and ridicule and cruelty, as Jesus experienced.

Sometimes people use the expression: "There'll be hell to pay". In the sufferings of Jesus we get an idea of what that really means. As we witness his sufferings, we're like tourists being given an insightful day-trip to hell. But wonderfully, because Jesus suffered this in our place, we don't have to go there.

For those who trust in him, this social price of sin has also been paid in full. And we can look forward to life in the ultimate community, the eternal city where God will live with his people. A place of love and harmony and peace. Instead of the shame and dishonour we deserve, we will enjoy glory and honour, because he suffered all that for us.

3. The spiritual suffering of Jesus
But there was more.

> And at three in the afternoon Jesus cried out in a loud voice, "*Eloi, Eloi lema sabachthani*" (which means "My God, my God, why have you forsaken me?"). *v 34*

On the cross Jesus didn't just *feel* forsaken by God. He really *was* **forsaken**. And this spiritual suffering was the ultimate agony for Jesus. At his baptism a voice from heaven had declared: "You are my Son, whom I love; with you I am well pleased" (Mark 1 v 11). But now, on the cross, the beloved Son became the object of God's righteous anger.

In one of the Exodus plagues darkness had covered the land of Egypt, and now the darkness of God's judgment covered the land of Israel for three hours from midday (Mark 15 v 33) as Jesus hung there, forsaken by God.

Why in God's salvation plan did Jesus have to suffer like this spiritually? Because that is part of the cost of sin. In his spiritual suffering he was paying the price for our sin.

We get a glimpse of this spiritual cost of sin in our world today. People alienated from God, without hope or purpose or meaning. But this spiritual cost of sin will again be seen most starkly in hell. Living in God's world now, we all enjoy so many blessings from him. Life, love, health, beauty, joy—they all come from the God who showers his gifts upon us.

But in hell the spiritual cost of sin will be experienced undiluted. A place of total alienation from God's goodness. Jesus described it as a place of "outer darkness", where the light of God's favour is never seen, but only the darkness of his righteous anger. A place of utter despair and futility and hopelessness.

But wonderfully, because Jesus suffered this for us, we don't have to. For those who trust in him, this spiritual cost of sin has been paid in full and the way into God's presence has been opened wide.

At the moment Jesus died, "the curtain of the temple was torn in two from top to bottom" (v 38). For centuries this heavy curtain in the temple had been a huge "no entry" sign, separating the people from God's presence in the Most Holy Place. Only the high priest had been able to enter, and only once a year. But at the moment Jesus died, God tore the curtain down. There was no longer any need for priests and sacrifices and temples. Instead, anyone who trusts in Jesus enjoys the presence of and intimacy with the Father through him. And we look forward to an eternal future in a place where "God himself will be with [us] and be [our] God" (Revelation 21 v 3).

When I was a kid I engraved the words "God is love" on a piece of wood which my mother still has. I actually burned the letters on with a large magnifying glass, sitting out in the sunshine one day. A magnifying glass gathers and focuses the sun's rays down to a small spot. And the heat of those focused rays is so intense that it can burn into wood.

On the cross it was as if a huge magnifying glass gathered the rays of God's judgment on the sins of millions and millions of God's people and focused them down on one spot—on his precious son, Jesus.

The true cost of living as we want

In this passage we get a breakdown of the cost of living as we want in God's world, and it is terrifyingly large. We see the cost physically, socially and spiritually in the sufferings of Jesus, as he picks up the bill for the sin of his people and pays it in full.

There were various responses to Jesus' crucifixion.

There was **Simon of Cyrene** (Mark 15 v 21)—a passing Libyan who was forced to carry the cross for Jesus.

Like him, some people's involvement with Jesus has been forced on them. Perhaps they were made to go to church when younger or to chapel at school, and they resent it and it's put them off.

Then there are **the soldiers** (v 24). For them it was a routine execution. Just another day in the office. They didn't see anything significant in the sufferings of this man. They were more interested in dividing up Jesus' clothes for their own profit. Like them, some people are just focused on doing their job and earning a living.

There were **the religious leaders** (v 31), mocking Jesus and his claim to be the Christ. Like them, many religious people dismiss Jesus and his claims.

Then there were **the bystanders** (v 35) who thought Jesus was calling Elijah, when in fact he was calling out to God. The words sound similar in Hebrew and Aramaic. Like them, many people have never really understood precisely *why* Jesus died. These bystanders even tried to keep Jesus alive by giving him sour wine to drink (v 36), waiting for Elijah to come to rescue him. For them it was just good entertainment. Similarly, some people just go along to church at Christmas and Easter for the show.

But at the end we read of a very different response:

> And when the centurion, who stood there in front of Jesus, saw how he died, he said, "Surely this man was the Son of God!"   *v 39*

When you get your credit-card bill in the post, someone has to pay. It won't go away just because you put it in the bin. Living as we want in God's world and ignoring him has a huge price tag. The question is: *who is going to pay?*

In the end we are left with a simple choice. Either we recognise Jesus for who he is and allow him to pay for us, or we pay for our sin ourselves in eternity. The sufferings of Jesus have given us some idea of the horror of that.

In a moral universe someone has to pick up the bill for my sin. It can't be a friend or loved one because they've got their own bill to sort out. The wonderful news of the gospel is that God is saying:

Give it to me. Let me pay. Jesus suffered for you to pay the price in full. Will you accept that?

That Jesus willingly endured such suffering for us tells us that we are more loved than we could have ever imagined. It also tells us that sin is a very, very big deal.

Knowing what it cost Jesus to pay the penalty for my sin should give me renewed determination to put sin to death in my life. Not to excuse it, or indulge it, but rather, to kill it.

And it tells us how blessed we truly are. In the sufferings of Jesus we get a glimpse of the eternal punishment from which we have been saved. And that is something for which we will be eternally grateful.

Isn't God's reaction to sin out of proportion to the crime?

When we look at the suffering of Jesus and the eternal suffering of hell, we may feel that God is overreacting in his punishment of sin. But first, as sinful human beings, we don't see sin the way God does. God is holy and hates it, whereas we often quite like it. Because we are sinners our sense of what is right and just is distorted.

Secondly, it is because sin is against God that it is so serious. As David said: "Against you, you only, have I sinned and done what is evil in your sight" (Psalm 51 v 4). Someone has explained it like this: "The gravity of the offence depends on the dignity of the one against whom it is committed." If we saw someone pulling a worm to pieces, we might be irritated at such a cruel, pointless way to treat a living creature. But we would not be appalled. If a cat were being mutilated, we would be much more upset and probably intervene, because in our scale of values a cat is a nobler animal than a worm. And if we saw someone torturing a child, we would be horrified and the memory would stay with us for ever. In every case the action would be the same, but against a different kind of being. Cutting a worm in two is not as bad as cutting a human in two. But how serious, then, must an offence be against God— the Creator, the Uncreated, who is far above all creatures? How can we begin to measure such appalling wrongdoing?

And thirdly, the punishment for sin in hell is never-ending because the sin of people in hell is never-ending. In hell there is no repentance from sin.

How can the eternal penalty of so many be paid in a few hours by just one man?

How could the suffering of one man pay the penalty owed by millions of people? And how could his suffering for just a few hours on the cross be an equivalent punishment to an eternity in hell, where, Jesus says, "the worms that eat them do not die, and the fire is not quenched" (Mark 9 v 48)?

We're never going to fully understand how this can be, because, as someone has said: "Finite minds, unsurprisingly, struggle to comprehend the mathematics of infinity!" But the answer is essentially to be found in who the one man is. Another person put it like this: "The value of Christ's sacrifice consists in the infinite worth of his own person". Jesus was not just another man. He is the eternal Word, who "was with God" and "was God" (John 1 v 1), who became flesh. "In Christ all the fulness of the Deity lives in bodily form" (Colossians 2 v 9).

Because of who he is, he has infinite worth, and his suffering has infinite worth. The "precious blood of Christ" (1 Peter 1 v 19) is of infinite value. And so on his own he is worth more than all people put together, and his suffering was able to pay for any number of people's sins. And because of his infinite worth, his suffering was infinite in value, although it lasted only a finite time. "By one sacrifice he has made perfect for ever those who are being made holy" (Hebrews 10 v 14).

Chapter 4

What did the cross achieve?

For me, Switzerland is up there as one of the most stunningly beautiful countries in the world. Snow-capped mountains, crystal-clear lakes, picture-postcard villages. What more could you want?

But the other day I was chatting to a Swiss guy. I asked him what it was like living there, and why on earth he would want to move away, as he had just done. He said: "Growing up there, you just don't notice. You sit on the train, commuting to work through the Swiss Alps. The tourists are going nuts with excitement, noses pressed against the windows, but you're just flicking through the newspaper or staring into space."

It can be a bit like that with the cross.

If you've grown up in a country where the cross is just part of the landscape, it's easy to take it for granted. All the more so if you grew up in a Christian home, or if you've been a Christian for many years. The cross is just part of the furniture. And it's maybe only when you see the reaction of someone appreciating it for the first time that you realise you've lost something.

One way to recover that sense of wonder is to take a closer look at what the cross achieved, and Romans 3 is a great place to go. Martin Luther described this passage as "the chief point ... and the very central place of the whole Bible".

> But now apart from the law the righteousness of God has been made known, to which the Law and the Prophets testify. This righteousness is given through faith in Jesus Christ to all who believe. There is no difference between Jew and Gentile, for all have sinned and fall short of the glory of God, and all are justified freely by his grace through the redemption that came by Christ Jesus. God presented Christ as a sacrifice of atonement, through the shedding of his blood—to be received by faith. He did this to demonstrate his righteousness, because in his forbearance he had left the sins committed beforehand unpunished—he did it to demonstrate his righteousness at the present time, so as to be just and the one who justifies those who have faith in Jesus.
>
> Where, then, is boasting? It is excluded. Because of what law? The law that requires works? No, because of the "law" that requires faith. For we maintain that a person is justified by faith apart from the works of the law. Or is God the

God of Jews only? Is he not the God of Gentiles too? Yes, of Gentiles too, since there is only one God, who will justify the circumcised by faith and the uncircumcised through that same faith. Do we, then, nullify the law by this faith? Not at all! Rather, we uphold the law. *Romans 3 v 21-31*

The justification of the sinner

The key, foundational, all-important thing which the cross achieves is our **justification**. Through the death of Jesus we are justified. "All have sinned and fall short of the glory of God, and all are justified freely by his grace" (v 23-24a). It's a really important word to understand if we are to grasp properly the meaning of the cross.

"Justified" was originally a legal term which meant to be acquitted—declared in the right—before a judge in a court of law. The opposite of being justified was to be condemned. So Deuteronomy 25 v 1 says the job of a judge is to justify the innocent and condemn the guilty.

Condemned before God's court

If you've ever been in a courtroom it was probably sitting in the spectator gallery, or on jury service, or as a witness or victim. Few of us will have appeared in court as the defendant. But one day *all of us will,* in the heavenly court, where God the Creator presides as judge. We'll be on trial for our lives. And the charge is outlined in Romans 3 v 23—"all have sinned and fall short of the glory of God".

Morally speaking, many people imagine humanity as spread over different floors of a skyscraper. On the very top floor you have the most moral or religious people in the world—the Mother Theresas and the like. Then on the next level down you have the great people who do a lot of good and give to charity. Then the floor with all the average people—who try their best, and don't make any spectacular messes. That's normally the floor most people think they live on. And below you are the used-car dealers, pushy sales people and grumpy grumblers. On the ground floor are the regular criminals. And then hidden away in the basement are paedophiles, mass murderers, and others whose crimes we deplore.

Most of us think that the way it works is that God draws a line somewhere on that moral spectrum. Most of us think that God accepts all those who live on our floor and above. You just make the cut.

But in reality there's only one floor. And everyone on it is condemned. Those we think have reached the pinnacle of moral courage and self sacrifice are just as condemned as those we believe to be utterly disgusting and reprehensible. Everyone, including you and me.

Because all of us, *without exception*, fall way, way short of the glory and perfection of God. And that is why the day of the trial is a frightening prospect, because it will be a "day of God's wrath, when his righteous judgment will be revealed" (Romans 2 v 5).

In the course of an average week lots of questions go through people's minds: "Where can I find a decent plumber?"; "What should I do with the rest of my life?"; "Did I shut the front door when I left the house this morning?"; "How can I get inner peace?"; "Where on earth is my wallet?" Not many are asking themselves the question: "How can I possibly be justified before God instead of condemned?" But it's the most important question we should be asking. As the guilty person that I am, how can I escape the coming judgment?

Justified by God's grace

The answer is right there in Romans 3 v 24. We are...

> justified freely by his grace through the redemption that came by Christ Jesus.

Being justified—declared in the right before God the Judge—is a gift from God through the cross of Christ. It's a result of grace—God's undeserved favour.

I was in a take-away restaurant the other day. A sign by the counter read: *Get a free bottle of soft drink, if you spend over £45.* My chicken chow mein came to £3.80, so it wasn't looking good. You don't get much for free in life. But our biggest need, to be justified before God, is met with a free gift from God.

And all we have to do is receive it. It is...

> to be received by faith.   *v 25*

Faith is simply coming to God with empty hands and saying thank you. "This righteousness [same word as "justification"] is given through faith in Jesus Christ to all who believe" (v 22). It's not that God does his bit and we help him out by doing our faith bit. This right standing with God is 100% from God and 0% because of our doing or deserving.

Imagine someone offered you a vast fortune, and they said that all you need is a separate account to put the money in. So you open a new account and the gift is transferred to you. Faith is exactly like opening an account to receive the money. We're not contributing anything. You wouldn't go around afterwards saying: "Well yes, this person did give me 10 million, but don't forget it was me that opened the account. I did my bit; I thoroughly deserved it!".

And wonderfully, if we have said yes to this free gift, we don't have to wait until the trial day to hear the verdict. Romans 5 v 1 says: "*since* we have been justified through faith". Past tense. It's already in the bag.

Some trials drag on for weeks, even months. The tension must be unbearable if you're the one on trial for your life, as you wait for that moment when the verdict is finally read out.

Some people live their whole lives with that tension as they wait for the Day of Judgment. Even believers. They *hope* the verdict is going to go their way, but they're *just not sure* if they've done enough. But Paul says that we are...

justified by faith *apart* from the works of the law.
Romans 3 v 28

If we trust in Jesus' death on the cross, we hear the verdict declared now: **"Justified"**. And if that's us, we should be punching the air and leaping for joy, like someone who was facing life in prison and has just walked free.

If you're acquitted in a court of law, you're declared innocent of the charges brought against you. But biblical justification is actually even better than that. It means being declared *righteous* before God—not just acquitted. A wonderful exchange has taken place.

> God made him who had no sin to be sin for us, so that in him we might become the righteousness of God. *2 Corinthians 5 v 21*

On the cross our sins were laid on Jesus and he paid for them, as though he had done them himself. God treated him as if he were the sinner. And as a result we enjoy the forgiveness of all our sins. "Everyone who believes in him receives forgiveness of sins through his name" (Acts 10 v 43).

But not only has our sin been paid for by Jesus, but his righteousness has been given to us. "Abraham believed God, and it was credited to him as righteousness" (Romans 4 v 3).

Jesus lived the perfect life. He always perfectly obeyed the Father, always did God's will, never sinned. That life of perfect obedience has now been credited to our account, with the result that, although we are still sinners, God sees us as being as righteous as Christ himself.

As one old hymn puts it: *Jesus, thy blood and righteousness, My beauty are, my glorious dress.* It's not just that the debt on our account with God has been cleared so we're left with a zero balance. Our account with God is now millions in credit!

This justification is the front-door key that gives us access to the house of God's blessings. The blessings that flow from justification are many and wonderful.

Peace with God

"Since we have been justified through faith, we have peace with God through our Lord Jesus Christ" (Romans 5 v 1). By nature we are God's enemies. Because of our sin, we are hostile to God and he to us. We're at war. But through the cross we are reconciled to God. "While we were God's enemies, we were reconciled to him through the death of his Son" (5 v 10). If anyone deserves a Nobel Peace Prize, it's the Lord God! He's brought this about.

And this peace with God brings peace within. There's an online community which brings people together who agree with the statement: *"I long to find inner peace and understanding"*. People leave their comments about inner peace. One person has simply written: "It's the only true thing I long for". Another says: "It's my goal to have peace in my life. I feel so anxious, so depressed, confused and lonely". Inner peace is clearly something people long to experience.

It is peace with God that brings peace within. Just before his death Jesus said to his disciples: "Peace I leave with you; my *peace* I give you" (John 14 v 27). The Bible says: "The fruit of the Spirit is love, joy, *peace...*" (Galatians 5 v 22). Peace with God through Jesus brings the peace of God into our hearts—and one day will bring peace to the whole universe.

At the cross the forces of evil were disarmed and defeated (Colossians 2 v 15). And at the return of Christ they will be finally overthrown. And then at last the universe will be at peace. God's ultimate plan is...

> through [Jesus] to reconcile to himself all things, whether things on earth or things in heaven, by making peace through his blood, shed on the cross.
> *Colossians 1 v 20*

There's a computer game called *The World Has Fallen Apart*, where you're given a map of the world in which the countries have been broken up into pieces. You have to click and drag the scattered fragments and put them back in their right place. It took me all of two minutes, after which a message flashed up: "Congratulations. You have mended the world!" Putting the real world back together is not quite so simple, but that is exactly what God will do through the cross.

Someone put it this way: "The reconciliation is cosmic in its ultimate accomplishments: the atonement of Jesus Christ washes to the four corners of the universe. By it a renewed heaven and a renewed earth have been guaranteed, and from it peace and union with God will flow for ever".

Adopted into God's family

But even reconciliation doesn't exhaust what the cross achieved. The Bible tells us that...

> the Spirit you received brought about your
> adoption to sonship. And by him we cry, "*Abba*,
> Father."   *Romans 8 v 15*

Those who trust in Jesus' death on the cross have been
adopted as children of God. In his classic book, *Knowing
God*, J. I. Packer writes this:

> *Adoption is the highest privilege that the gospel
> offers: higher even that justification ... To be right
> with God the judge is a great thing, but to be
> loved and cared for by God the Father is a greater.*

He goes on:

> *I am a child of God. God is my Father; heaven is my
> home ... Say it over and over to yourself first thing
> in the morning, last thing at night, as you wait for
> the bus, any time when your mind is free, and ask
> that you may be enabled to live as one who knows
> it is utterly and completely true ... This is the Chris-
> tian's secret of ... a God-honouring life.*

The justice of God

The dilemma of justice

All this is fantastic, but there is a problem. In justifying
us God is letting the guilty go free. That isn't just! As we
have already seen, the job of a judge is "acquitting the
innocent and condemning the guilty" (Deuteronomy
25 v 1)—but God is acquitting the guilty. Proverbs 17

v 15 says: "Acquitting the guilty and condemning the innocent—the LORD detests them both". So God is doing what he says he hates, because he is justifying the guilty. Romans 4 v 5 even describes God as the one who "justifies the ungodly". In Exodus 23 v 7 God says very plainly: "I will not acquit the guilty"—and yet that is precisely what God is doing in justifying sinful people like you and me. He's declaring us in the right before him, even though our sins are piled up to heaven.

Imagine a paedophile is charged with the sexual abuse and murder of dozens of young children. The prosecution's case is flawless. DNA evidence makes it virtually 100% certain that he is guilty. And then the judge delivers a verdict of "not guilty". A great moment for the defendant, perhaps, but a terrible day for society.

There would be gasps of horror in the courtroom. The papers would be screaming for justice the next morning, and demanding the resignation of the judge and a retrial. Justice has not been done. The judge is corrupt, immoral. He has acquitted the guilty. If that would be an outrage in an earthly courtroom, how much more so in the heavenly one.

Is there an unrighteous judge sitting on the throne of the universe? If so, we are no better off than the citizens of a country ruled by a corrupt dictator. We might as well have Stalin running the universe—and what a terrifying prospect that would be.

And if that is what God is like, he's got no moral right to sit as judge on anyone at the end of time. He himself needs to be on trial.

The display of justice

The answer to this problem is found in *how* we are justified. Romans 5 v 9 says: "We have now been justified *by his blood*". It is the cross that makes all the difference in the world. It means God hasn't turned a blind eye to our wrongdoing. He's paid for it himself in the death of Jesus in our place. To help us understand this the apostle Paul takes us out of the courtroom to two other places in town.

Redemption

First, he takes us to the marketplace—the world of business and commerce. We are justified "through the redemption that came by Christ Jesus" (Romans 3 v 24). **Redemption** is a commercial word that means "setting free through the payment of a price".

In the Old Testament you could redeem a slave, securing their freedom by paying a price. The Bible says we are slaves to sin and death, but we have been redeemed through the death of Jesus. His death was the ransom through which we have been set free. He came "to give his life as a ransom for many" (Mark 10 v 45). There's no dodgy dealing. It's all above board.

The Bible tells us we are redeemed through the cross.

Atonement

Secondly, the apostle Paul takes us to the temple, the place of sacrifice. "God presented Christ as a sacrifice of atonement, through the shedding of his blood" (Romans 3 v 25). A sacrifice of atonement—or "propitiation" as some translations put it—is a sacrifice that turns aside God's righteous anger. In Jesus, God himself provided that sacrifice. He hasn't just swept our sins under the carpet.

Many people, even within the church, don't like this idea of Jesus' death being a sacrifice to turn aside God's wrath. They claim it's what you find in pagan religion—people trying to placate the angry gods with their offerings.

But what the Bible is talking about is very different. In pagan religion sacrifices are needed because the "gods" are moody and bad-tempered, but in the Bible it's because the holy God is rightly angry at sin.

In pagan religion it's *people* who do the appeasing, but in the Bible God does it *himself*.

In pagan religion people *bribe the gods* with food or human sacrifice, but in the Bible *God gave himself* in the person of his Son.

In Christ, God took the punishment we deserve on himself. In the death of Jesus Christ on the cross we see the full extent of God's commitment to justice. God is perfectly just in justifying sinners. As the passage we started with in this chapter says:

> He did this to demonstrate his righteousness, because in his forbearance he had left the sins committed beforehand unpunished—he did it to demonstrate his righteousness [same word as "justice"] at the present time, so as to be just and the one who justifies those who have faith in Jesus.
> *v 25b-26*

Imagine being in a huge open-air theatre at night. You are just one of tens of thousands of people there. The lights dim, a hush descends, and all attention is drawn to the stage by a single bright spotlight. And then you hear the voice of God himself thundering from heaven: "Now I will reveal myself to you in all my glory".

A murmur of anticipation goes round the auditorium as they prepare themselves. Will it be a blinding light? Will it be a terrifying vision of a massive, powerful God who could not be contained even in this, the largest auditorium on earth? What will he look like?

The curtain is slowly raised. And on the stage the spotlight picks out the naked, bleeding figure of a man nailed to a cross.

As the time of his death approached, Jesus said: "Now the Son of Man is glorified and God is glorified in him" (John 13 v 31). It is on the cross that the glory of what God is truly like is revealed. The character of God sparkles like a precious diamond as the Son of God hangs there. The cross displays God's love, his mercy, his wisdom, his power, and his justice. Through the cross God justly justifies the unjust.

The signs of health

Here are two signs that we are spiritually healthy and have a good grasp of the cross.

1. Humilty

First, my attitude to God will be one of humility.

Where, then, is boasting? It is excluded.

Romans 3 v 27

If I've grasped the cross, I won't come to God carrying all my good deeds and saying: "Hey, get a load of this performance: church attendance, Bible knowledge, good deeds. It's all there. Check it out!" Instead I'll come empty-handed. *Nothing in my hands I bring. Simply to the cross I cling.* I will recognise both my own unworthiness and the wonder of his grace.

2. Accepting others

A second healthy sign will be my attitude to others—I will accept as fellow Christians all those God has made into his sons and daughters.

> Is God the God of Jews only? Is he not the God of Gentiles too? Yes, of Gentiles too, since there is only one God. *v 29-30a*

In the church in Rome, Christians of Jewish background were looking down on Christians of non-Jewish background. But in his letter to them, Paul points out to them that the cross means we all enter *through the same door.* Realising this is the key to accepting and loving one another.

Sometimes we look up at other Christians and feel inferior and inadequate, because they are so gifted and knowledgeable. Or we look down on other Christians and feel superior—perhaps because they've sinned in the past in ways we would never dream of, or because of the struggles they still have. But the cross is the great leveller. If we are saved, it is by grace alone through faith alone. God has done it all. And he's done it through the cross.

How can an event so long ago affect me today?

Romans 5 v 12-19 compares and contrasts Adam and Christ. It explains how what they both did so long ago has profound implications for every generation born on earth.

Because Adam was our representative and head of the human race, his one act of disobedience in Eden at the beginning of history has affected every person who has ever lived. Through that one act, sin and death entered the world and we were "made sinners" (v 19). By nature all of us are *in Adam*—born sinners and so under God's wrath.

But Jesus came as "the last Adam" (1 Corinthians 15 v 45), the representative and head of a new humanity. And through his righteous act on the cross, instead of condemnation and death, now justification and life flow to all who are "in Christ" (Romans 8 v 1-2).

This union with Christ is not automatic. It is by grace, through faith, that we become united with Christ and one with him. This is something the Holy Spirit makes possible. The most common description of the Christian in the New Testament is someone who is "in Christ"—united with him (Romans 16 v 7; 2 Corinthians 12 v 12).

It is through this union with Christ that we receive all

the blessings secured for us on the cross (Ephesians 1 v 3-14). In marriage two become one, and what belongs to each is shared with the other. So if a very poor woman who is massively in debt marries a billionaire, all her debts become his, and his wealth becomes hers. And so with us and Christ! Through union with Christ, my sin and guilt were credited to him and he paid for it on the cross; his perfect obedience and righteousness were credited to my account, and I rejoice in it. "God made him who had no sin to be sin for us, so that in him we might become the righteousness of God" (2 Corinthians 5 v 21).

If Jesus died for my sins, why do I still feel guilty?

As Christians, we need to take the truth of what Christ has done for us and apply it to our own experience, so that we believe it in our minds and feel it to be true in our hearts. Sometimes we know in our heads—*Christ has paid for all our sins and I've been forgiven*—but we don't feel it. Having faith means believing this is true and enjoying the grace in which we stand. And we need to be specific in applying it to ourselves.

If you feel guilty, ask God by his Spirit to put his finger on the particular sin. Confess that sin to God and turn from it. Acknowledge that Christ has died for that sin and thank God for that. Take a Bible verse about what Christ has done and take God at his word. Ask God to help you *feel* that truth applied to this particular sin.

You could maybe sing through a hymn or song praising God for what Christ has done. It's as we take God at his word that we experience a cleansed conscience. Hebrews 10 v 22 encourages us to *"draw near to God ... with the full assurance that faith brings, having our hearts sprinkled to cleanse us from a guilty conscience"*.

One writer put it like this: "We must take trouble to purge and cleanse our consciences with the blood of Christ. If we find that we have sinned, we must run straightaway to the blood of Christ to wash away our sin. We must not let the wound fester, but get it healed immediately. As we sin daily, so he cleanses daily, and we must daily go to him for it ... Be sure with each day to clear the sin of the day. Then shall our consciences have true peace."

If you've done that and your conscience is still troubled, it could be that you are not repenting of sin. Christ did not die for us so we can just keep on sinning with a clear conscience. We do need to repent. And where we've wronged others, we need to put that right, by saying sorry to them and making amends where possible.

Or it may be that you still feel guilty because you have an over-sensitive conscience. Sometimes a Christian may be worried about things that the Bible does not actually condemn—perhaps extra rules that we feel under compulsion from our upbringing to obey. The solution is to go back to the Bible. As Luther said: *"My conscience is captive to the Word of God"*. We need to keep shaping our consciences by the word of God, and trusting that the death of Jesus cleanses us from all sin.

Chapter 5

How should we respond to the cross?

Grand Central in New York is regarded by many as the world's loveliest station. It's also the world's largest railway station in terms of platforms, having 44 platforms serving 67 tracks. It was previously called Grand Central Terminal because all railway lines ended there.

In each of us there is a Grand Central hub—the place from which all the traffic of our life radiates out. For some, that hub is the desire to be liked or loved. Their need for affirmation is their primary motivating factor. For others, it is the pursuit of perfection. They can't admit weakness or failure, and everyone else falls short of their standard. For some, it is the desire for a comfortable lifestyle, financial security and prestige. For others, it is the determination to leave their mark on the world and make a difference.

In each of us there is a Grand Central Station from which the thousands of trains of our actions and thoughts and emotions depart and to which they eventually return. *What is it for you?* And what should it be for the Christian?

The Bible would no doubt put more than one thing in Grand Central, but the cross would certainly be there. The apostle Paul said: "May I never boast except in the cross of our Lord Jesus Christ" (Galatians 6 v 14), and: "I resolved to know nothing while I was with you except Jesus Christ and him crucified" (1 Corinthians 2 v 2). Someone has said:

> *Paul's whole world was in orbit around the cross. It filled his vision, illumined his life, warmed his spirit. He gloried it in. It meant more to him than anything else. Our perspective should be the same.*

But what does this look like in practice?

1. Trust in the cross

Jesus' death for us is the only basis on which we can ever be right before God. We're saved by grace alone through faith alone, not by works. "For it is by grace you have been saved, through faith … not by works, so that no one can boast" (Ephesians 2 v 8-9).

A good test of whether your trust at the moment is in Christ and his death, or in yourself and your performance, is *assurance*. Suppose you were to die right now, reading this book. As your eyes close in death, are you certain that God will accept you? If your answer is: *I hope so, but you can never know*, that is a sign you're trusting in your own goodness. If you trust in Christ's death, you know for sure.

If God said to you, as you stood before him later today: *Why should I accept you?*, what would you say?

- *Because I've lived a good life?*

- *Because I've tried my best?*

- *Because I'm better than many others and have been regular at church?*

Each of those responses would show that you are trusting in your own goodness—which can never save you.

The only right response is: *I'm a sinner, but I trust in Jesus who died for me.* Galatians 2 v 16 says: "A person is not justified by works of the law, but by faith in Jesus Christ ... by the works of the law no one will be justified." If my trust is in Christ's death I can have complete confidence that God accepts me now, and will welcome me when I die (Romans 5 v 8-9).

As we go on in the Christian life, we need to beware shifting our confidence from the cross to ourselves. It happened in the Galatian churches and it can happen to us just as easily. They had started well but then had been taken in by people who said that trusting in the cross is not enough—you need also to do this or that to be accepted by God. We mustn't start relying on our performance as Christians as the reason for our acceptance by God. We mustn't start operating as if God accepts us because we're managing to keep all the Christian plates spinning by having a daily devotional time, attending church, serving in some way at church, taking communion regularly, or getting along to a Bible study group.

And we mustn't start relying on our feelings, as if God accepts us when we feel close to him, but not when we don't. How we feel is not necessarily what is real.

It's why regularly taking communion can be helpful to us, not because we are put right with God through it, but so we constantly remember to refocus on the basics—that it is *only* through Jesus' broken body and shed blood that we are saved.

2. Wonder at the cross

Generally in life it's said that as you grow older you tend to lose the sense of wonder you had as a child. But we mustn't lose our sense of wonder at the cross.

Paul didn't. You can feel his sense of wonder when he says: "I live by faith in the Son of God, who loved me and gave himself for me" (Galatians 2 v 20). We too need that.

Sometimes when things go wrong and life is hard, we're tempted to doubt whether God really loves us. And when we look at the sin in our own hearts we may be tempted to despair and feel: *How could anyone love me, knowing what I'm really like?* But when we look at the cross we find the answer: "The Son of God ... loved me and gave himself for me". And that is a love from which nothing can separate us (Romans 8 v 35, 39).

Perhaps at this very moment you're feeling weighed down with the burden of guilt. The memory of something you said or did is like a heavy backpack that you're carrying around. It leaves you feeling weary and low. The message of the gospel is simple: *Check in your baggage!* You know that sense of relief at the airport when you finally leave at the check-in desk the bags you've been lugging around. Do the same with your burden of guilt. Don't carry it around any longer.

Why not check it in right now, confessing your sin to God, turning from it, leaving it at the cross, and thanking God for his grace? "It is God who justifies. Who then is the one who condemns?" (Romans 8 v 33-34). Don't wallow in guilt—wonder at the cross!

3. Take up the cross

> Then [Jesus] said to them all: "Whoever wants to be my disciple must deny themselves and take up their cross daily and follow me".   *Luke 9 v 23*

To take up our cross means publicly to identify ourselves with Christ—to be known as a follower of Jesus and not to be ashamed of it; to put up with the rejection that it may bring. Hebrews 13 v 13 urges us to: "go to [Jesus] outside the camp, bearing the disgrace he bore". Jesus warned: "If they persecuted me, they will persecute you also" (John 15 v 20). As someone has put it, "Mission sooner or later leads into passion [in the sense of suffering] ... The very shape of mission is cruciform".

There's a song they sing in the house churches in China. The chorus goes:

To be a martyr for the Lord,
To be a martyr for the Lord,
I am willing to die gloriously for the Lord.

The verses are a gruesome and graphic account of how the apostles suffered and died. Then the final verse concludes:

I am willing to take up the cross and go forward,
To follow the apostles down the road of sacrifice.
That tens of thousands of precious souls can be
   saved,
I am willing to leave all and be a martyr for the
   Lord.

It's a bit different to many of the songs we sing in our church! Sometimes people who've got noisy neighbours, or a boss who is a pain in the neck say: ... *but we all have our crosses to bear*. That is not what Jesus meant.

Carrying your cross doesn't just mean putting up with some inconvenience. It means following Christ openly whatever the cost. Being known as his follower; living for him, and taking the hit; enduring the shame, wherever that leads.

Taking up your cross is not the path of self-fulfilment. It is the path of self-denial. Jesus warns us: "Whoever wants to be my disciple must deny themselves and take up their cross daily and follow me". If I'm living for myself and to make my life now comfortable and easy, I can't be a follower of Jesus; I won't take up my cross. Taking up your cross and denying yourself go hand in hand. Denying yourself is not about giving up chocolate for Lent. It's about saying no to a life with your own comfort at the centre, and instead following Christ whatever the cost.

So we're to trust in Christ's cross, but we are also to take up our own cross. Not to atone for our sins—Christ has done that—but to follow him. This is the cost of true discipleship. Someone summed it up like this:

> *Like Barabbas we escape the cross—*
> *like Simon we carry it.*

Both are true. And taking up our cross is a daily discipline. "Whoever wants to be my disciple must deny themselves and take up their cross *daily* and follow me".

There are a number of things you do each day—wash, eat, sleep. So every day we are to deny ourselves, take up our cross and follow Christ. As you head out each day and you take your handbag or man-bag with you, take up your cross as well. Say to yourself: *I am a follower of Christ. Today I will follow him, live for him and speak for him, whatever the cost.* And if you find wearing a cross on your lapel is a helpful reminder of that, go for it!

4. Live out the cross

Romans 6 v 6 says: "We know that our old self was crucified with him so that the body ruled by sin might be done away with, that we should no longer be slaves to sin". Through faith we are united with Christ in his death and resurrection. What happened to him has happened to us.

When you get on a plane, what happens to the plane happens to you. It takes off, so you take off. Where it goes, you go. And so through faith we are "in Christ". When you became a Christian, you "got in the plane", and what happened to Christ happened to you. When he died, you died. Your old self, your old life, is now history. And you have been raised with Christ to live a new life. And so we are to live differently, saying no to sin and yes to godliness.

So next time you're tempted to pass on some juicy gossip, or selfishly to insist on your own plans for the weekend, or to click on some pornographic website, or to switch TV channels to a violent film—stop and say to yourself: *No! That old life was crucified with Christ and is now gone. I'm a new person now!* And do something loving and pure in its place.

5. Look to the cross

Gandhi said: "I could accept Jesus as a martyr, an embodiment of sacrifice, and a divine teacher. His death on the cross was a great example to the world."

Tragically, as far as we know, Gandhi didn't trust in the cross as the sacrifice for his sins. For him, the cross was just an example. But if we do *trust* in the cross, we must also *look* to the cross. It is the pattern and example for us to follow. The cross is the supreme example for us of loving service; of putting the interests of others before our own; of sacrifice for the sake of others.

As Jesus hung on the cross, it's as if he said: *Look and learn. This is how to serve. This is what love looks like. Now you try. Lay down your life for another. Serve the other. Stop just looking to your own interests. I've set you an example for you to copy. You'll be blessed if you do it.*

The cross is the pattern for all our relationships. "Live a life of love, just as Christ loved us and gave himself up for us" (Ephesian 5 v 2). We are to love with cross-like love in all our relationships.

Love like this in the church

We're to serve one another as Christ served us. Jesus said:

> Whoever wants to be first must be slave of all. For even the Son of Man did not come to be served, but to serve, and to give his life as a ransom for many. *Mark 10 v 44-45*

When you don't feel like serving others—having people other than your good friends round for meals, going to your fellowship group even though you're tired, helping out at the youth group even when the kids are driving you nuts, speaking to that person at church on his own when you'd rather hang out with more fun people —when you feel like that, where do you look for motivation? *Look to the cross.*

> This is how we know what love is: Jesus Christ laid down his life for us. And we ought to lay down our lives for our brothers and sisters.
> *1 John 3 v 16*

Laying down our lives is not about making a futile gesture—rather, like Jesus' death, it is deliberate, determined love in action. Giving money to provide basics for poor Christians in other countries; supporting those in our own church family who are needy; going round to see the widow who is on her own, and mowing her lawn; making food for the mother who's just given birth; visiting the person who's been taken into hospital; sending a card to encourage someone who's finding life tough. This is cross-shaped living.

Love like this in the home

Are you preparing for marriage? Or do you want to improve and renew your marriage? *Then look to the cross.*

> Husbands, love your wives, just as Christ loved the church and gave himself up for her.
>
> *Ephesians 5 v 25*

Love as Christ loved. If you have young kids, occasionally it happens that in the middle of the night one of them will start crying! As a parent, at that moment you have a choice—you can leap out of bed before your spouse does, or you can say to yourself: *If I keep very, very still, I can pretend to be asleep.* No prizes for working out what the cross-shaped response is!

Give yourself up for your spouse. Ask them how you can make their daily life easier, and love and support them better, and do it. Find out their love-language, and speak it!

Love like this in the world

Do you want your life to be fruitful for God? *Look to the cross.* Jesus said:

> Unless a grain of wheat falls to the ground and dies, it remains only a single seed. But if it dies, it produces many seeds.   *John 12 v 24*

He was speaking not just of his own death, but also of the life of discipleship. As with Jesus, so with us. It is as we die to self that we bear fruit, being known as Christ's followers, serving the gospel and the needs of others.

Luther used a Latin phrase, *incurvatus in se,* which means "curved inward on oneself". That is the shape of our lives by nature; our mindset and focus is turned in on ourselves. But by God's grace, our lives become increasingly cruciform—cross-shaped; our hands stretched out to God and to others.

Such living is costly but fruitful.

And when we feel the cost, and are given a hard time for being a Christian, again we're to look to the cross and be encouraged by Christ's example: "When he suffered, he made no threats. Instead, he entrusted himself to him who judges justly" (1 Peter 2 v 23).

6. Pass on the cross

Finally, the message of the cross is too good to keep to ourselves. *Pass on the cross.* The apostle Paul said:

> We preach Christ crucified: a stumbling-block to Jews and foolishness to Gentiles, but to those

whom God has called, both Jews and Greeks,
Christ the power of God and the wisdom of God.
1 Corinthians 1 v 23-24

The cross is a stumbling-block to Jews—that is, religious people are offended to be told that they too are sinners who need rescuing. The cross is foolishness to Gentiles—that is, other people just find the very notion absurd that someone dying on a cross gets us right with God.

But "Christ crucified" was the very heart of Paul's message, because he knew that the cross was the only thing that had the power to save sinful people. And so we need to tell people about the cross. It's fine to talk about church or God, but at some point the person needs to hear the amazing news that Jesus died for their sins, and that this is how they can get right with God and escape the coming judgment.

Such a message is the very opposite of self-promotion. It's not flattering to the self, either in us or in them. It's not just saying: *You're a wonderful person and God has a wonderful plan for your life*. It's not just saying: *You have a God-shaped hole in your life and God can fill it*. God's message is humbling. And that is why some will resist and reject it.

But it's also the message God uses to save those he has chosen. And we need to have confidence in that. So pray for opportunities for people to hear the message of the cross. And why not learn a gospel outline such as *Two Ways to Live*, so you can better explain the message of the cross yourself when the opportunity comes up.

Count von Zinzendorf was the founder of the 18th-century Moravian Christian community and missionary movement. As a 19-year-old he found himself in an art gallery in Germany, standing in front of a painting called *Ecce Homo* (Behold the man!). It showed Christ wearing the crown of thorns. Underneath, the inscription read:

All this I did for you. What do you do for me?

The young count was deeply challenged, and there and then asked the crucified Christ to use his life to serve God. More than a hundred years later the hymnwriter Frances Havergal sat before the same painting and was similarly moved. She wrote the hymn *I gave my life for thee*. Focusing on the cross, meditating on it, is a life-changing experience. It moves us to trust in Christ's death and to give ourselves in his service. If you're weighed down by sin and guilt, come to the cross. If you're lacking zeal and motivation in the Christian life, come to the cross. If you're just living for yourself, come to the cross.

What we mustn't do is just walk away. The journalist Malcolm Muggeridge wrote of one period in his life:

I would catch a glimpse of the cross—and suddenly my heart would stand still. In an instinctive, intuitive way I understood that something more important … was at issue than our good causes, however noble they might be … I should have worn it … It should have been my uniform, my

*language, my life. I shall have no excuse; I can't
say I didn't know. I knew from the beginning, and
turned away.*

That is the one thing we mustn't do.

Did Jesus die for everyone?

On the cross, did Christ pay the penalty for the sins of
everyone (what some people call general redemption),
or only of those who would ultimately be saved (particular redemption)?

There are many Bible verses where a plain reading suggests that Jesus' death has a universal scope—"for the
whole world"—even though it may only be *effective*
for those who put their trust in him.

Those who argue for particular redemption, point out
that there are ways of reading these verses which suggests otherwise. For example, Jesus said he would die
specifically for his sheep, in a passage where he explicitly says some of his hearers are *not* his sheep (John
10 v 11, 26). He died for "his friends" (John 15 v 13),
and for "the church" (Acts 20 v 28; Ephesians 5 v 25).
These people are those whom the Father has chosen,
given to Jesus and will draw to him (John 6 v 37, 44).
When Paul says that God gave up his Son "for us all",
he defines these people in the next verse as "those
whom God has chosen" (Romans 8 v 32-33).

Christ's death did not just make salvation *possible* for
everyone, but actually *secured* the salvation of his people. If Christ's death *did* pay for the sins of everyone,

surely everyone would be saved (which the Bible clearly says isn't the case), because how could God be fair in demanding that people pay again for their sins in hell when Christ has already paid for them? It would be double payment for sin. It would also mean that Christ's intention to save everyone would be in conflict with the Father's decision to choose only some.

Passages that speak of Christ dying "for the world" can be understood as referring to sinners generally. "God so loved the world that he gave his one and only Son" (John 3 v 16) is the same as saying that God so loved sinners that he gave his Son. "The world" is humanity in rebellion against God. "God was reconciling the world to himself in Christ, not counting men's sins against them" (2 Corinthians 5 v 19) does not mean every single person in the world is reconciled to God, but just that sinners generally are.

When Jesus said that through his death he would "draw all people to [himself]" (John 12 v 32), he meant all without distinction (all kinds of people), not all without exception (every person who has ever lived). All people without exception haven't come to him, but all *types* of people have, which is something the early Christians found shocking.

When 1 Timothy 2 v 4 says that God "wants all people to be saved", it is in the same sense that he wants all people to stop being selfish and unloving. That is his "moral will". But this doesn't mean that in his "sovereign will" he will bring about the salvation of everyone. Sometimes God allows bad things to happen to serve a higher end (as with the cross, which was a wicked act by sinful men, but according to God's sovereign plan,

Acts 2 v 23). The highest end of all is his glory (Romans 9 v 22-24).

Bible-believing Christians differ on this question of who Christ died for, but we agree on the need for everyone to *hear* the gospel. We do not know who the people are whom God has chosen and for whom Christ died, and so we are to make the gospel offer to *all* people, assured that no one who wants to come to Christ will be turned away (John 6 v 37).

How can I keep the cross central in my life?

I don't just need to be telling the good news about Jesus to those who don't yet know him—I need to be telling it to myself each day! This involves daily facing up to my own sinfulness before God, and taking on board personally what Jesus has done for me on the cross.

Some find the acronym "**Jesus' SCARS**" a help in doing this:

- You start by meditating on the person of Jesus.

- **S is for sin**—ask God to make you aware of your sin and confess that to him.

- **C is for the cross**—take your sins to the cross, remembering that it is through Christ alone that you are accepted by the Father.

- **A is for adoration**—praising God for his love in sending the Lord Jesus to die for us.

- **R is for responsive reading**—reading the Bible and turning it into a conversation with God.

- **S is for supplication**—asking for needs to be met for yourself and others.

Another provision to keep us cross-centred is the Lord's Supper. Jesus said: "Do this in remembrance of me" (1 Corinthians 11 v 24, 25).

He could have told us to do something to remember his birth, or resurrection, or ascension, or the pouring out of the Spirit at Pentecost, but he didn't. It's his death he wants us to remember above all else, and so he told us to remember him in the eating of bread and drinking of wine.

As we share these symbols, we re-centre ourselves on the cross, and we feed again on Christ in our hearts by faith.

By the same author

What happens when I die?
by Marcus Nodder

We all have questions about death. Despite the strong assurance the Bible gives us about life beyond the grave, Christians are often troubled by other questions. What will happen on the day of judgment? Will we have bodies in heaven? Will there be rewards?

This short, simple book is designed to help Christians understand what God has said about these questions in the Scriptures.

Making work work
by Marcus Nodder

Most of us spend most of our waking hours working—in a factory, at the office, or at home. It can be fulfilling, but is often frustrating. Yet we are often a little confused about the point of work, other than to earn money.

The eight studies in this Good Book Guide for small groups or individuals, outline what the Bible says, exciting and challenging us about God's perspective on our work in his world.

Order from your local Good Book website:
UK & Europe: www.thegoodbook.co.uk
North America: www.thegoodbook.com
Australia: www.thegoodbook.com.au
New Zealand: www.thegoodbook.co.nz

Other titles in this series

Did the devil make me do it?
by Mike McKinley

When Jesus walked the earth, he cast out demons and had powerful encounters with the devil. But who exactly is the devil, and where did he come from? And what is he up to in the world today? This short, readable book explains clearly and simply what we can say with certainty from the Bible about Satan, demons and evil spirits.

Who on earth is the Holy Spirit?
by Tim Chester and Christopher de la Hoyde

Many people find it easy to understand about God and Jesus, but struggle to understand quite how and where the Holy Spirit fits into the picture. Who exactly is he? And how does he work in our lives? These short, simple books are designed to help Christians understand what God has said in the Bible about these questions and many more.

Order from your local Good Book website:
UK & Europe: www.thegoodbook.co.uk
North America: www.thegoodbook.com
Australia: www.thegoodbook.com.au
New Zealand: www.thegoodbook.co.nz